The BIG BOOK of
cello songs

ISBN 978-1-4234-2672-1

Visit Hal Leonard Online at
www.halleonard.com

Contact Us:
Hal Leonard
7777 West Bluemound Road
Milwaukee, WI 53213
Email: info@halleonard.com

In Europe contact:
Hal Leonard Europe Limited
42 Wigmore Street
Marylebone, London, W1U 2RN
Email: info@halleonardeurope.com

In Australia contact:
Hal Leonard Australia Pty. Ltd.
4 Lentara Court
Cheltenham, Victoria, 3192 Australia
Email: info@halleonard.com.au

CONTENTS

ALL MY LOVING
from A HARD DAY'S NIGHT

CELLO

Words and Music by JOHN LENNON
and PAUL McCARTNEY

ALL THE SMALL THINGS

CELLO

Words and Music by TOM DE LONGE
and MARK HOPPUS

Bright driving Rock

ALLEY CAT

CELLO

By FRANK BJORN

ANOTHER ONE BITES THE DUST

CELLO

Words and Music by
JOHN DEACON

Steady Rock

To Coda ⊕ | 1.

2.

D.C. al Coda   **CODA** ⊕

AMERICA
from the Motion Picture THE JAZZ SINGER

CELLO

Words and Music by
NEIL DIAMOND

Moderately

small notes optional

ANY DREAM WILL DO

from JOSEPH AND THE AMAZING TECHNICOLOR® DREAMCOAT

CELLO

Music by ANDREW LLOYD WEBBER
Lyrics by TIM RICE

BE TRUE TO YOUR SCHOOL

CELLO

Words and Music by BRIAN WILSON
and MIKE LOVE

Slowly

BAD DAY

CELLO

Words and Music by
DANIEL POWTER

Moderate groove

D.S. al Coda

CODA

BARELY BREATHING

CELLO

Words and Music by
DUNCAN SHEIK

(It's A)
BEAUTIFUL MORNING

CELLO

Words and Music by FELIX CAVALIERE
and EDWARD BRIGATI, JR.

BEAUTY AND THE BEAST

from Walt Disney's BEAUTY AND THE BEAST

CELLO

Lyrics by HOWARD ASHMAN
Music by ALAN MENKEN

Moderately slow

BEYOND THE SEA

CELLO

Words and Music by CHARLES TRENET,
ALBERT LASRY and JACK LAWRENCE

Slowly

BLACKBIRD

CELLO

Words and Music by JOHN LENNON
and PAUL McCARTNEY

Slowly and smoothly

BLUE SUEDE SHOES

CELLO

Words and Music by
CARL LEE PERKINS

BOOGIE WOOGIE BUGLE BOY
from BUCK PRIVATES

CELLO

Words and Music by DON RAYE
and HUGHIE PRINCE

THE BRADY BUNCH

Theme from the Paramount Television Series THE BRADY BUNCH

CELLO

Words and Music by SHERWOOD SCHWARTZ
and FRANK DEVOL

BUTTERFLY KISSES

CELLO

Words and Music by BOB CARLISLE
and RANDY THOMAS

BREAKING FREE

from the Disney Channel Original Movie HIGH SCHOOL MUSICAL

CELLO

Words and Music by
JAMIE HOUSTON

Moderately

CABARET
from the Musical CABARET

CELLO

Words by FRED EBB
Music by JOHN KANDER

CALIFORNIA DREAMIN'

CELLO

Words and Music by JOHN PHILLIPS
and MICHELLE PHILLIPS

CANDLE IN THE WIND

CELLO

Words and Music by ELTON JOHN
and BERNIE TAUPIN

CHIM CHIM CHER-EE

from Walt Disney's MARY POPPINS

CELLO

Words and Music by RICHARD M. SHERMAN
and ROBERT B. SHERMAN

Lightly, with gusto

small notes optional

CLOCKS

CELLO

Words and Music by GUY BERRYMAN, JON BUCKLAND,
WILL CHAMPION and CHRIS MARTIN

(They Long to Be)
CLOSE TO YOU

CELLO

Lyric by HAL DAVID
Music by BURT BACHARACH

COLORS OF THE WIND
from Walt Disney's POCAHONTAS

CELLO

Music by ALAN MENKEN
Lyrics by STEPHEN SCHWARTZ

small notes optional

COME FLY WITH ME

Cello

Words by SAMMY CAHN
Music by JAMES VAN HEUSEN

COPACABANA
(At the Copa)
from Barry Manilow's COPACABANA

CELLO

Music by BARRY MANILOW
Lyric by BRUCE SUSSMAN and JACK FELDMAN

DO-RE-MI
from THE SOUND OF MUSIC

CELLO

Lyrics by OSCAR HAMMERSTEIN II
Music by RICHARD RODGERS

DO WAH DIDDY DIDDY

CELLO

Words and Music by JEFF BARRY
and ELLIE GREENWICH

(Sittin' On)
THE DOCK OF THE BAY

CELLO

Words and Music by STEVE CROPPER
and OTIS REDDING

DON'T BE CRUEL
(To a Heart That's True)

CELLO

Words and Music by OTIS BLACKWELL
and ELVIS PRESLEY

DON'T LET THE SUN GO DOWN ON ME

CELLO

Words and Music by ELTON JOHN
and BERNIE TAUPIN

Slow Rock

DON'T SPEAK

CELLO

Words and Music by ERIC STEFANI
and GWEN STEFANI

D.S. al Coda

CODA

small notes optional

DRIFT AWAY

CELLO

Words and Music by
MENTOR WILLIAMS

Moderately fast

DUKE OF EARL

CELLO

Words and Music by EARL EDWARDS,
EUGENE DIXON and BERNICE WILLIAMS

THEME FROM E.T. (THE EXTRA-TERRESTRIAL)

from the Universal Picture E.T. (THE EXTRA-TERRESTRIAL)

CELLO

Music by
JOHN WILLIAMS

EDELWEISS
from THE SOUND OF MUSIC

CELLO

Lyrics by OSCAR HAMMERSTEIN II
Music by RICHARD RODGERS

EVERY BREATH YOU TAKE

CELLO

Music and Lyrics by
STING

EVERYTHING IS BEAUTIFUL

CELLO

Words and Music by
RAY STEVENS

FALLIN'

CELLO

Words and Music by
ALICIA KEYS

FIELDS OF GOLD

CELLO

Music and Lyrics by
STING

FLY LIKE AN EAGLE

CELLO

Words and Music by
STEVE MILLER

Moderately, in 2

FOR ONCE IN MY LIFE

CELLO

Words by RONALD MILLER
Music by ORLANDO MURDEN

FOREVER YOUNG

CELLO

Words and Music by ROD STEWART,
JIM CREGAN, KEVIN SAVIGAR and BOB DYLAN

FUN, FUN, FUN

CELLO

Words and Music by BRIAN WILSON
and MIKE LOVE

Bright Rock

THE GIRL FROM IPANEMA
(Garôta de Ipanema)

CELLO

Music by ANTONIO CARLOS JOBIM
English Words by NORMAN GIMBEL
Original Words by VINICIUS DE MORAES

GOD BLESS THE U.S.A

CELLO

Words and Music by
LEE GREENWOOD

GONNA BUILD A MOUNTAIN

from the Musical Production STOP THE WORLD – I WANT TO GET OFF

CELLO

Words and Music by LESLIE BRICUSSE
and ANTHONY NEWLEY

GOODBYE YELLOW BRICK ROAD

CELLO

Words and Music by ELTON JOHN
and BERNIE TAUPIN

GREEN GREEN GRASS OF HOME

CELLO

Words and Music by
CURLY PUTMAN

HAPPY DAYS
Theme from the Paramount Television Series HAPPY DAYS

CELLO

Words by NORMAN GIMBEL
Music by CHARLES FOX

HAVE I TOLD YOU LATELY

CELLO

Words and Music by
VAN MORRISON

HEART AND SOUL
from the Paramount Short Subject A SONG IS BORN

CELLO

Words by FRANK LOESSER
Music by HOAGY CARMICHAEL

Moderately, lightly rhythmical

HOGAN'S HEROES MARCH
from the Television Series HOGAN'S HEROES

CELLO

By JERRY FIELDING

HERE WITHOUT YOU

CELLO

Words and Music by MATT ROBERTS,
BRAD ARNOLD, CHRISTOPHER HENDERSON,
and ROBERT HARRELL

Moderate Rock

I DREAMED A DREAM
from LES MISÉRABLES

CELLO

Music by CLAUDE-MICHEL SCHÖNBERG
Lyrics by ALAIN BOUBLIL, JEAN-MARC NATEL
and HERBERT KRETZMER

Music and French Lyrics Copyright © 1980 by Editions Musicales Alain Boublil
English Lyrics Copyright © 1986 by Alain Boublil Music Ltd. (ASCAP)
Mechanical and Publication Rights for the U.S.A. Administered by Alain Boublil Music Ltd. (ASCAP) c/o Spielman Koenigsberg & Parker LLP,
Richard Koenigsberg, 1745 Broadway, New York NY 10019, Tel 212-453-2500, Fax 212-453-2550, ABML@skpny.com

I HEARD IT THROUGH THE GRAPEVINE

CELLO

Words and Music by NORMAN J. WHITFIELD
and BARRETT STRONG

I SAY A LITTLE PRAYER

CELLO

Lyric by HAL DAVID
Music by BURT BACHARACH

I WHISTLE A HAPPY TUNE

from THE KING AND I

CELLO

Lyrics by OSCAR HAMMERSTEIN II
Music by RICHARD RODGERS

Brightly

I WILL REMEMBER YOU
Theme from THE BROTHERS McMULLEN

CELLO

Words and Music by SARAH McLACHLAN,
SEAMUS EGAN and DAVE MERENDA

I WRITE THE SONGS

CELLO

Words and Music by
BRUCE JOHNSTON

I'M POPEYE THE SAILOR MAN

Theme from the Paramount Cartoon POPEYE THE SAILOR

CELLO

Words and Music by
SAMMY LERNER

IF I EVER LOSE MY FAITH IN YOU

CELLO

Music and Lyrics by
STING

IMAGINE

CELLO

Words and Music by
JOHN LENNON

Medium slow

IT'S MY LIFE

CELLO

Words and Music by JON BON JOVI,
RICHARD SAMBORA and MARTIN SANDBERG

Moderately

IT'S STILL ROCK AND ROLL TO ME

CELLO

Words and Music by
BILLY JOEL

Moderately fast Rock Shuffle

JAILHOUSE ROCK

CELLO

Words and Music by JERRY LEIBER
and MIKE STOLLER

JOY TO THE WORLD

CELLO

Words and Music by
HOYT AXTON

JUMP, JIVE AN' WAIL

CELLO

Words and Music by
LOUIS PRIMA

KANSAS CITY

CELLO

Words and Music by JERRY LEIBER
and MIKE STOLLER

KOKOMO
from the Motion Picture COCKTAIL

CELLO

Words and Music by MIKE LOVE, TERRY MELCHER,
JOHN PHILLIPS and SCOTT McKENZIE

Moderately bright

To Coda

1.

2.

D.S. al Coda

CODA

LET 'EM IN

CELLO

Words and Music by
PAUL and LINDA McCARTNEY

LET'S STAY TOGETHER

CELLO

Words and Music by AL GREEN,
WILLIE MITCHELL and AL JACKSON, JR.

LIKE A ROCK

CELLO

Words and Music by
BOB SEGER

LIVIN' LA VIDA LOCA

CELLO

Words and Music by ROBI ROSA
and DESMOND CHILD

Fast, with a steady beat

LOVE AND MARRIAGE

CELLO

Words by SAMMY CAHN
Music by JAMES VAN HEUSEN

LOVE STORY
Theme from the Paramount Picture LOVE STORY

CELLO

Music by FRANCIS LAI

MAGGIE MAY

CELLO

Words and Music by ROD STEWART
and MARTIN QUITTENTON

Moderately bright

MAKING OUR DREAMS COME TRUE

Theme from the Paramount Television Series LAVERNE AND SHIRLEY

CELLO

Words by NORMAN GIMBEL
Music by CHARLES FOX

MAYBE I'M AMAZED

CELLO

Words and Music by
PAUL McCARTNEY

Moderately

small notes optional

MICHELLE

CELLO

Words and Music by JOHN LENNON
and PAUL McCARTNEY

MICKEY MOUSE MARCH

from Walt Disney's THE MICKEY MOUSE CLUB

CELLO

Words and Music by
JIMMIE DODD

Brightly

MISSION: IMPOSSIBLE THEME
from the Paramount Television Series MISSION: IMPOSSIBLE

CELLO

By LALO SCHIFRIN

MISTER SANDMAN

CELLO

Lyric and Music by
PAT BALLARD

MOON RIVER

from the Paramount Picture BREAKFAST AT TIFFANY'S

CELLO

Words by JOHNNY MERCER
Music by HENRY MANCINI

MY HEART WILL GO ON
(Love Theme from 'Titanic')
from the Paramount and Twentieth Century Fox Motion Picture TITANIC

CELLO

Music by JAMES HORNER
Lyric by WILL JENNINGS

Moderately

MY WAY

CELLO

English Words by PAUL ANKA
Original French Words by GILLES THIBAULT
Music by JACQUES REVAUX and CLAUDE FRANCOIS

NA NA HEY HEY KISS HIM GOODBYE

CELLO

Words and Music by ARTHUR FRASHUER DALE,
PAUL ROGER LEKA and GARY CARLA

ON BROADWAY

CELLO

Words and Music by BARRY MANN,
CYNTHIA WEIL, MIKE STOLLER and JERRY LEIBER

PEPPERMINT TWIST

CELLO

Words and Music by JOSEPH DiNICOLA
and HENRY GLOVER

POCKETFUL OF MIRACLES

CELLO

Words by SAMMY CAHN
Music by JAMES VAN HEUSEN

Moderately, with a lilt

PUFF THE MAGIC DRAGON

CELLO

Words and Music by LENNY LIPTON
and PETER YARROW

PUT YOUR HAND IN THE HAND

CELLO

Words and Music by
GENE MacLELLAN

QUIET NIGHTS OF QUIET STARS
(Corcovado)

CELLO

English Words by GENE LEES
Original Words and Music by ANTONIO CARLOS JOBIM

ROCK AROUND THE CLOCK

CELLO

Words and Music by MAX C. FREEDMAN
and JIMMY DeKNIGHT

ROCK WITH YOU

CELLO

Words and Music by
ROD TEMPERTON

SATIN DOLL

CELLO

By DUKE ELLINGTON

SAVE THE BEST FOR LAST

CELLO

Words and Music by PHIL GALDSTON,
JON LIND and WENDY WALDMAN

THEME FROM "SCHINDLER'S LIST"

from the Universal Motion Picture SCHINDLER'S LIST

CELLO

Music by JOHN WILLIAMS

SHE WILL BE LOVED

CELLO

Words and Music by ADAM LEVINE
and JAMES VALENTINE

SING
from SESAME STREET

CELLO

Words and Music by
JOE RAPOSO

Moderately

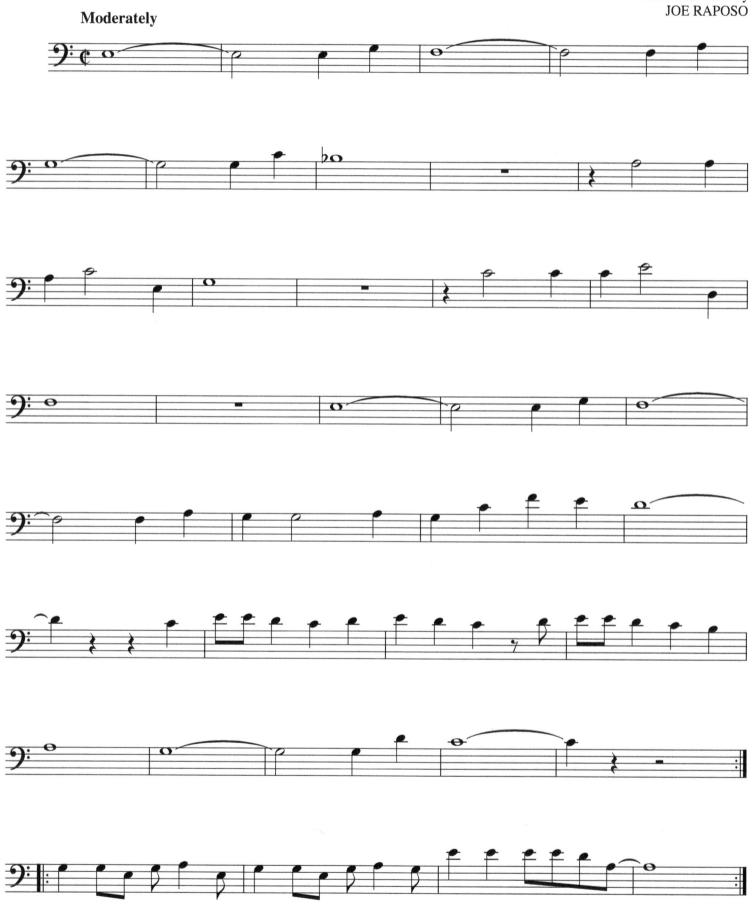

SO LONG, FAREWELL
from THE SOUND OF MUSIC

CELLO

Lyrics by OSCAR HAMMERSTEIN II
Music by RICHARD RODGERS

SOMEWHERE OUT THERE

from AN AMERICAN TAIL

CELLO

Music by BARRY MANN and JAMES HORNER,
Lyrics by CYNTHIA WEIL

SPANISH FLEA

CELLO

Words and Music by
JULIUS WECHTER

STACY'S MOM

CELLO

Words and Music by CHRIS COLLINGWOOD
and ADAM SCHLESINGER

Medium Rock

SUNRISE, SUNSET
from the Musical FIDDLER ON THE ROOF

CELLO

Words by SHELDON HARNICK
Music by JERRY BOCK

TAKE MY BREATH AWAY
(Love Theme)
from the Paramount Picture TOP GUN

CELLO

Words and Music by GIORGIO MORODER
and TOM WHITLOCK

THAT'S AMORÉ
(That's Love)
from the Paramount Picture THE CADDY

CELLO

Words by JACK BROOKS
Music by HARRY WARREN

THIS LAND IS YOUR LAND

CELLO

Words and Music by
WOODY GUTHRIE

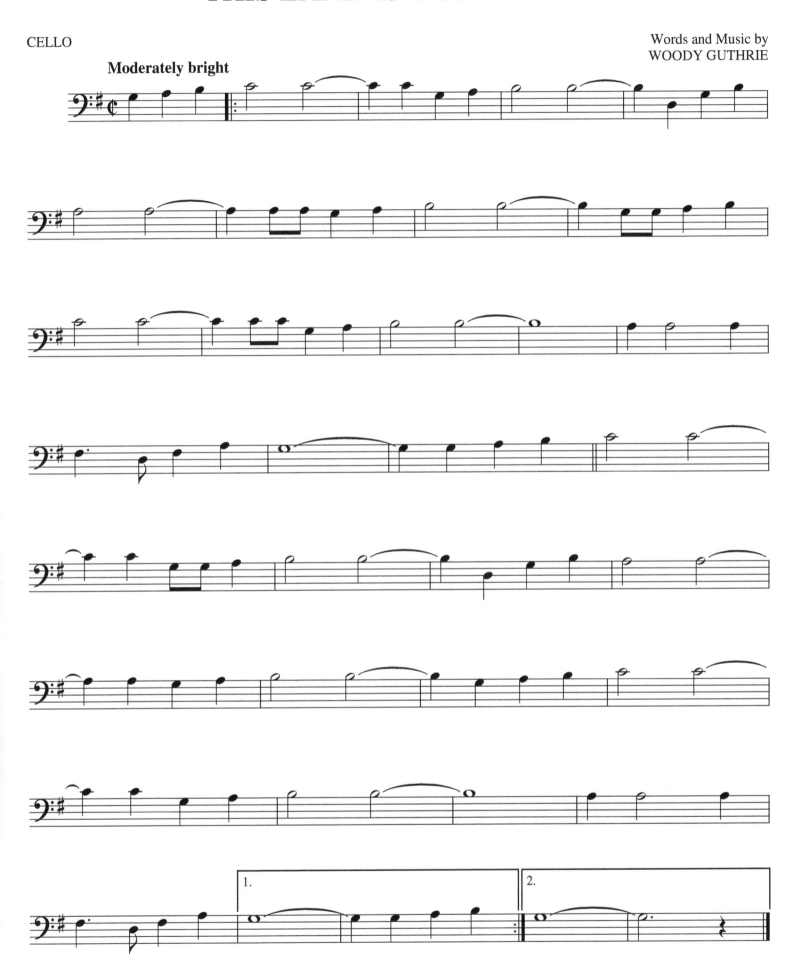

THOSE WERE THE DAYS

CELLO

Words and Music by
GENE RASKIN

TIME AFTER TIME

CELLO

Words and Music by CYNDI LAUPER
and ROB HYMAN

A THOUSAND MILES

CELLO

Words and Music by
VANESSA CARLTON

Moderately fast

small notes optional

To Coda

1.

TOMORROW
from the Musical Production ANNIE

CELLO

Lyric by MARTIN CHARNIN
Music by CHARLES STROUSE

Moderately slow

TOP OF THE WORLD

CELLO

Words and Music by JOHN BETTIS
and RICHARD CARPENTER

TWIST AND SHOUT

CELLO

Words and Music by BERT RUSSELL
and PHIL MEDLEY

UNCHAINED MELODY

CELLO

Lyric by HY ZARET
Music by ALEX NORTH

UNDER THE BOARDWALK

CELLO

Words and Music by ARTIE RESNICK
and KENNY YOUNG

Moderately, with a beat

UNITED WE STAND

CELLO

Words and Music by ANTHONY TOBY HILLER
and JOHN GOODISON

THE WAY YOU MOVE

CELLO

Words and Music by ANTWAN PATTON,
PATRICK BROWN and CARLTON MAHONE

WE ARE THE WORLD

CELLO

Words and Music by LIONEL RICHIE
and MICHAEL JACKSON

WE BELONG TOGETHER

CELLO

Words and Music by MARIAH CAREY,
JERMAINE DUPRI, MANUEL SEAL, JOHNTA AUSTIN,
DARNELL BRISTOL, KENNETH EDMONDS, SIDNEY JOHNSON,
PATRICK MOTEN, BOBBY WOMACK and SANDRA SULLY

Slow Soul

WHAT THE WORLD NEEDS NOW IS LOVE

CELLO

Lyric by HAL DAVID
Music by BURT BACHARACH

WITH A LITTLE HELP FROM MY FRIENDS

CELLO

Words and Music by JOHN LENNON
and PAUL McCARTNEY

WONDERFUL TONIGHT

CELLO

Words and Music by
ERIC CLAPTON

WOOLY BULLY

CELLO

Words and Music by
DOMINGO SAMUDIO

YELLOW SUBMARINE

CELLO

Words and Music by JOHN LENNON
and PAUL McCARTNEY

YOU ARE THE SUNSHINE OF MY LIFE

CELLO

Words and Music by
STEVIE WONDER

YOU RAISE ME UP

CELLO

Words and Music by BRENDAN GRAHAM
and ROLF LOVLAND

Moderately slow

small notes optional

YOU'VE GOT A FRIEND

CELLO

Words and Music by
CAROLE KING

ZIP-A-DEE-DOO-DAH

from Walt Disney's SONG OF THE SOUTH
from Disneyland and Walt Disney World's SPLASH MOUNTAIN

CELLO

Words by RAY GILBERT
Music by ALLIE WRUBEL